Bayna Bayna
In-Between
بين
بين

Zeina Azzam

A Publication of The Poetry Box®

Poems ©2021 Zeina Azzam
All rights reserved.

Editing & Book Design by Shawn Aveningo Sanders
Cover Design by Shawn Aveningo Sanders
   (derived from photo by Ryan Gerard)
Author Photo by Jeff Norman

No part of this book may be reproduced in any manner
whatsoever without permission from the author, except
in the case of brief quotations embodied in critical essays,
reviews and articles.

ISBN: 978-1-948461-84-9
Printed in the United States of America.
Wholesale Distribution via Ingram.

Published by The Poetry Box®, 2021
Portland, Oregon
ThePoetryBox.com

*To my parents, Samih and Alice Azzam
—refugees, immigrants, constant travelers
in-between*

Note:

Bayna in Arabic means "between," and bayna bayna roughly translates as "betwixt and between." It reflects the feeling of being in-between identities, between home and exile, between childhood and adulthood, between wholeness and loss, between living and dying...somehow always in-between. Using the Arabic words bayna bayna is a nod to my Arab heritage—as I live in my American home. Combining these Arabic words with the English "in-between" speaks of a dual identity, a bicultural and bilingual view of the world that is bewildering, enriching, and beautiful, all at the same time.

Contents

In-Between Home and Exile
Colors for the Diaspora ... 9
A Syrian Refugee Speaks ... 10
Syrian Refugee at the Dental Clinic ... 11
After 93 Years ... 12
My Father Is Now a Memory ... 13
Crossing the Mediterranean ... 15
Syria's Disappeared ... 16
Leaving My Childhood Home ... 18
Immigrant ... 19
Non-Lieux ... 21
Khayr ... 22
Bayna Bayna, In-Between ... 23

In-Between Losing, Learning, Loving
My Father's Hands ... 27
Bob Hennessy, 1955-1974 ... 28
Far Side of the Moon ... 29
Learning to Make a Bed ... 31
Diving In ... 33
Losses ... 35
End of a Marriage ... 37
My Mooring ... 38
Poem for an Empty House ... 39
Lingerings ... 40
Dinnertime ... 41
Unexpected Gifts ... 42
Waiting ... 43
Traveling with the Speed of Light ... 44

Acknowledgments 47
About the Author 49
About The Poetry Box® 50

بين بين

*In-Between
Home and Exile*

Colors for the Diaspora

Blue-green watery globe
tugging to a red core
we are a distant comet,
white cloud of unburnished rocks,
frisking the heavens
for an arc
to earth, sea, home.

Green-brown Palestine,
cactus fruit and wild thyme,
olive orchards, cypress trees…
we travel on your mountain tops
tethered by voices from suitcases
and the yaw of blackened keys.

Blue-black night
silver stars of ancestors
traveling a displaced orbit
around a lost sun, repeating:
when will we see the colors of our land,
when will we land….

A Syrian Refugee Speaks

To you, I am the story
on the evening news.
My charcoal mane braids mystery
with fear, my words push eyes
to narrow, backs to rise.
Others dole out largesse at borders
to me, a wingless bird to feed.
You note my brown skin, imagine
my kin as the reclining odalisques
in Delacroix's painting, the boy
charming a snake in Gerome's.
My life is a tale of once-upon-a-time,
a thousand and one ruses,
myth and mirror fused
by the heat of the hell of war.

To me, I am the history book
and the poem, the suckling
and the breast, the amulet
locating paradise, al-janna:
it lies at the feet of mothers.
Now our country is an empty womb,
tales of fleeing tattooed in our skin,
white flags carried out of houses,
buried in rubble. Each time I beseech
the crescent moon for a blessed month,
I seek signs of stone houses and
olive trees left behind. I wait
for the morning that will bring back
mothers' milk, a scent of jasmine,
the dignity of home.

Syrian Refugee at the Dental Clinic

Eman from Homs is 20 years old.
At 13 she married and got pregnant
with the first of four children.

A broken tooth and three cavities,
baby on her breast,
mouth wincing in pain.

Eman never learned to use a toothbrush
to clean accumulated tar, plaque,
or microscopic bits of food

left over from her journey a month ago.
Maybe that's why she clenches
her teeth, to keep the taste of home.

After 93 Years

~to my mother

Your body has withered, a once supple fruit
plump and smooth, now desiccated by the fires

of years—the crippling fear of war, a young
bride fleeing, hoisting a baby and a suitcase

of clothes, a key, what gold you could wear,
traversing a burning country then another

wondering if you would ever see the sea
at Haifa again. The Mediterranean left its trace

in everything from then on: olives and figs, cedar
trees, a turquoise necklace, dresses in azure blue,

watery sunsets and opposing moons. But your
yearnings, upended so many times that now

you are always afraid—of a pebble underfoot,
the possibility of rain, a slight wheeze, back

aches that keep you awake. Even knocks
on the door make your shoulders clench, seize.

So you summon the good years, carry them
like badges in embroidered purses, opened

for the world to see, the thin skin of your hands
barely covering delicate blue veins. There are

no tears, as if stones are allegories for hearts, and
so much slips away, slowly, as your body wanes.

My Father Is Now a Memory

My father is now a memory —
dreamlike, clinging, fleeting,
rooted.
I will nurture it as he nurtured his plants:
babies in a cradle, rocking gently.

The roses in the garden mourn,
He loved us, we loved him.
The figs stand still
wishing for his tenderness.
My father searched for Palestine in them,
the memory of sweetness reawakened,
nostalgia guiding him homeward.

I can't remember him as a younger man anymore.
He is an old man with clouds for hair,
crevices in the earth of his face,
a waterfall nose, crescent moon smile.
He would sing snippets of a song,
recite a line of poetry.
Sometimes it would make sense,
sometimes it was out of place.
He might laugh heartily, amused by a memory.

He tried to teach my children to lick
a drop of coffee from his little finger
as he had done with me on his lap decades ago.
He clung to memories,
found solace in reliving, replicating.
Maybe he could find a home for the old in the new.

My father yearned for the homeland
he saw again only once in fifty years.
We should never have left,
he would say out of the blue, shaking his head.

[. . .]

بين 15 بين

They shot your neighbor,
it was wartime,
the Deir Yassin massacre had just come to light.
No matter: we should have stayed.

Maybe he would have been killed, too.
Maybe I would never have been born:
a fig tree cut down, a fig imagined.

Fifteen roses he bought the day before he died,
planted only three.
My mother gave the others away to friends, one by one.
They will yearn for him,
be planted far from home,
refugees in diaspora.
He loved us, we loved him.

Crossing the Mediterranean

How do we overcome war and poverty only to drown in your sea?
—Jehan Bseiso, "No search, no rescue"

You step onto the brown earth
where water seeped between grains of sand
and disappeared as if without a country.

You remember how in its infancy
hydrogen and oxygen clasped together
with no argument, in early love,

making communities in the faraway blue.
Maybe it was a fiery birth, thunder and sparks,
like your journey's start.

Now under your feet
the ground goes from soft to hard,
now welcoming, now not.

You look for signs, hold your children,
wait for rain—
even a dim drizzle will see you

collecting drops in your mind's cistern
to be sure they last. You must wash your feet,
make weak tea until you can return.

Syria's Disappeared

~for Jamil

The day you disappeared it rained,
drops evaporated, no trace.
We searched anyway
in Homs and Aleppo, Damascus,
even on the altar of Baal in Palmyra
where you imagined baptizing your son.

I remember you conjuring the story
of the cheeks—*turn and forgive like Jesus*,
you said. But the war demanded more,
blood owed like currency.
Under the barrel bombs, body parts
flew into the government's banks—

ears, eyes, hands, cheeks filling coffers
like a butcher shop's scraps.
We prepared white shrouds
and prayed, we who beseech God
in everyday speech, under domes
and by the candlelit icon

in your mother's house.
You accepted this indulgence of hers
because death always hid behind the door.
It took her and your sister, too, as if with mercy
and now we wonder, what happened to
those icons of the Virgin Mary, of St. George,

the Last Supper—anything with a door to
loved ones, to you. Outside, fists were shouting:
al-shaab yureed—the people want—
isqat al-nidham—to bring down the regime...
but tongues were cut, people herded
into trucks driven to another horizon.

At first we stayed to wait for you
even as children started wetting their beds again.
Priests offered no solace in holy bread and wine.
Imams stayed home on Fridays.
What were your last thoughts?
Where is your body?

Leaving My Childhood Home

On our last day in Beirut
with my ten years packed in a suitcase,
my best friend asked for a keepsake.
I found a little tin box
to give her, emptied of lemon drops,
that would hold memories of our childhood:
us swinging in the dusty school yard,
rooftop hide and seek,
wispy-sweet jasmine,
kilos of summertime figs,
King of Falafel's tahini-bathed sandwiches,
our pastel autograph books.
All those remembrances
crammed in that box,
tiny storytellers waiting to speak.
Later her family would uproot too,
transplant like surly Palestinian weeds
pulled every few years.
We all knew about this,
even the kids.
I never saw her again
but know that she also
learned to travel lightly,
hauling empty boxes
pulsing with kilos
of memories.

Immigrant

I grew up eating cheese with bitter olives,
sesame and thyme-infused olive oil
on warm bread.
Names in my family all meant something
like lifelong challenges:
beautiful, splendid, victorious, forgiving.
In my childhood books
words flowed from right to left,
direction didn't matter then.

At ten we traveled east to west
against time. I gained seven hours
of youth, lost my compass:
in New York, no sea
to swallow the sun each day.

Foods were sweet in America.
People spoke as fast as they walked.
Everything was large: washing machines,
supermarkets, even bananas and red grapes.
We settled in this vast, cold place
with neither boots nor a sense of
how to be warm.
Snowfalls were beautiful and cruel,
the freezing air slapped our faces
each morning.

Inside there was the smell of garlic and onions
on the stove, loud talking over the phone
with relatives overseas.
My family inhaled and exhaled
politics like cigarettes, all the time.
We blamed the British, the Americans,
Arab leaders, Zionists, communists,
or a history that was simply unkind.

[. . .]

The TV in the background reported news
in a language we spoke
but did not really understand.
All this over a good meal, always,
as if the hunger was in our bellies
and not in our hearts.

Non-Lieux

It was at the bookstore that
I understood. You held my hand,
explained Augé's theory of the non-place.
Like waiting at the elevator,
roaming the airport:
we make our own place
in those gray-colored non-places.

The world felt like a null space then.
Fixing ourselves here and there—
negatives in positives—
nothing else mattered.

After you left I saw the tragedy
of this theory, the now fraught space
we created. You even called it
a dangerous place.
We became solitary refugees
just like our parents,
climbing back to the non-places
in-between, landless
with no landing.

Khayr

From the time farmers rise with the sun
until night descends, there is talk of it—
songs and Qur'anic verses about khayr,
morning of khayr, evening of khayr.
There is no getting around goodness.

Tisbahi ala khayr, my mother would wish
me as she kissed my forehead at bedtime:
may you wake up to goodness. Later I learned
to respond: *w'inti min ahlo*, may you be
part of its family—the family of khayr.

Even watching TV, as we waited for bad
news from Gaza, she would admonish,
khayr inshallah! Goodness, God willing!
No matter the misfortune, she was sure Allah
would eventually bring khayr to Palestine.

Maybe it all started with her neighbors
in Jaffa, the family whose name was
Khayrallah, God's goodness. From kindness
to comity, their ancestors packed so much
in this name: it was a hedge against hardship,

an incantation in their bones—Palestine's
bones—where khayr resides from morning
till night, in a mother's kiss at bedtime, deep
in a farmer's land. There, the roots of khayr
multiply in the earth, goodness bristling.

Note: *Khayr* is the Arabic word for "goodness."

Bayna Bayna, In-Between

To be the first generation in this country, with another culture always looming over you, you are the ones who are born homeless, Bedouins.... You're torn in two. You get two looks at the world. You may never have a perfect fit, but you see far more than most ever do.
—Diana Abu-Jaber, *Arabian Jazz*

Through a darkened window
I look for the moon of my childhood.
It was bigger then, closer
with rays spread like illumined hands
against a deep blackness
between night and morning.
After we crossed the sea
then the ocean
leaving home behind
I began to see everything
like this moon's light,
bayna bayna, in-between,
bookended by other elements,
defined by borders not its own—
I was a green shoot
sprouting from two leaves,
a river meandering between banks
that spell its shape, give it a name.
My dreams were flower petals
pressed in pages of a book
about aliens and travelers.
I lived in the canyon
between a mother language
and an adopted tongue,
bayna bayna, betwixt and between…
I looked for others who collect stories
about childhood moons,
oceans crossed with faith

[. . .]

that we will press against each other
on the other side,
make something new: two eyes
wide open, two looks
at the world, lifting up our
in-between-ness
not knowing if one day
we would see far more
than most ever do.

بين بين

*In-Between
Losing, Learning, Loving*

My Father's Hands

They were not large, but thick
fleshy workers in the garden
nursing eggplants and fennel,
okra and chard,
digging and tilling and weeding,
making the soil an obliging host.

Maybe that's what made
his fingers rough in spots,
or maybe it was the constant leafing
through books: a loving lick
and a flip-flap of the page
in search of nuggets
that would be turned over and over
in his mind.

After he died
I found bookmarks between pages
carefully pointing
like tags next to seedlings in the earth:
These are the plants I hoped for.
These are the ideas that made me grow.

Bob Hennessy, 1955-1974

You rode through our high school years
on a ten-speed, not fast, but deliberate, bold,
arms wide — two erect branches seeking sunlight —
palms outstretched to greet air.

To you everything had a pithy core to explore,
scattered seeds needed to be gathered,
beheld, unpeeled, understood.
As our classmates went to college
you hitchhiked west, baled hay,
befriended folks none of us would ever meet.

You towered at six-four, a robust trunk,
flaming red curls standing up to the world:
soldiers at attention.

Maybe that's why I think of you most in autumn
when the Japanese maple turns myriad shades of flame.
I imagine your roots lie here,
leaves fall as if in deference.
The year you died winter came too soon.

Far Side of the Moon

"Her face is as beautiful as the moon."
—Old Arab saying

She is my mother
though the nugget
of who she used to be
is now turned away from us
like the far side of the moon,
reflecting light somewhere else.

My mother pauses at
now-elusive words
forgets how to do simple things
like changing the TV channel,
making coffee,
reading more than a few lines
of a library book.

We talk every day about
the same things
and reminisce, too, because
she loves to remember her life
before the moon shifted.

My mother is slowly letting go
of her things—the pans and spatulas
left behind like disinvited guests,
the dough hook and wire whip,
laborers for decades,
reluctantly given away.
Stained glass butterflies hovering
on her living room window
have alighted elsewhere.

Left in cabinets now are pieces
she can't forsake. Tapestries and
bowls from Palestine that remind her
of scarlet poppies, a cobalt blue sea.
An oversize tin box stuffed with
black and white photographs
from before the war,
a sentry for her memories.

She has not let go of that war —
but the war doesn't linger much
anymore on her lips
because my mother now ends
conversations before it's time,
gives up on finishing a sentence.

Yet her cratered face,
still beautiful, is illumined
by visits of a grandchild,
telephone calls, a son's embrace.
We bring chocolates, elicit a smile
that lingers a while.
My mother reminds us
to look for the moon,
even if turned, even if dark.

Learning to Make a Bed

My mother taught me how to make a bed
when I was so young I could barely reach
the mattress while standing. We would walk
from side to side to pull and push the unruly
sheets and make sure the blanket was tucked
over everything—like a protective father,
I imagined. Of course, neither my father nor
my brothers ever made their beds because
it was women's work. And so I was taught
what women did and didn't do early on.
I followed my mother's movements in the
kitchen and accompanied her to buy bananas
and grapeleaves and rice. She showed me how
to pick stones out of bowls of lentils and beans.
I imitated my mother as she made Arabic coffee
on the stove then offered trays of sweets to guests.
We decorated cookies with jagged-edged
tweezers to make patterns in the dough.
During olive season we sat on the floor with hammers,
smacked each olive to open it before pickling.
I watched my mother chop and place cucumbers
and eggplants in brine. Together we picked leaves
of *mulukhiyyeh* from oversize green bouquets
my father brought home from the souk. In my
girls' school I was shown how to place a wooden
egg in a sock for darning, sew a button, even
embroider with bright threads—all before I was
ten years old. With brothers much older, I had
no idea what boys learned each day. But I wanted
to be like them and run around the house without
a shirt. I did that one day when I was seven and
everyone smiled smugly at me, as if I would learn
on my own not to do it again. And I learned.
Like making a bed, I figured out what should
be covered and tucked in and out of sight,

[. . .]

how to make things right and good, that these ordinary acts were daily reminders of something that was bigger, one I didn't yet understand.

Note: *Mulukhiyyeh* is a type of dark green leafy mallow popular in many countries of the Middle East and North Africa.

Diving In

Imagining the feeling deep below
this linear surface, which curves
with every move, small breath

I let go and let my body venture
down beneath the thin horizon,
easily pierced

Skin, at first taut,
remembers that in deep ocean
there is comfort in the absence

of lines and angles.
Like that I soften, disappear
into the silence of water

Maybe this is peace—the end
of self and beginning
of collectiveness,

an undisturbed flow
after shedding mirrors, photographs,
the burdens of colorful clothing

We let muscles unlax, slacken,
spreading buoyant limbs
in expectation of languishing

in this hushed realm
—or of rising to the surface,
for it takes little to alter

our fluid, fragile dance
(a mouth unclosed, a secret
disclosed, a gathering wind,

[. . .]

the albatross in waiting,
hesitations reclaiming their homes)
reminding me to search

for light air that seemed
so far away, gasping
for the oxygen that pulls us apart.

Losses

1.
All those nights we didn't make love
add up to years:
I mourn them in the morning
when a bright sun slaps me awake,
at night under the moon's muted light,
a white lily at a funeral.

2.
Surveying Beirut's cityscape, my eyes trip over
bullet holes and craters in buildings
trying desperately to see things whole.
Purple flowers gather
between cracks, abandoned optimists.
People here age faster,
their hair and nails grow
with a silent knowing.

3.
Nothing really surprises me anymore:
the preacher has an extramarital affair,
the homeless guy in the park
types on a laptop
by his overfull shopping cart.
I once read about a butterfly
that befriended a man, coming back
to see him every day for weeks.
Even planets look like they backtrack
in orbit, as if remembering they left
something behind.

[. . .]

بيـن 35 بيـن

4.
The lost amulet came from Sanaa's
deep labyrinth of sellers and stalls.
Silver hammered in a circle of geometry,
floral and radiating. A sun on my breast.
I wore it like a dog tag: if I die, then please
remember me by this loveliness.
Now I curse the weak link
in that forgotten chain.

5.
After we sign the divorce papers
will we simply shut the door
of that chamber in our hearts?
Or will we keep one hand down and fisted,
the other open to the sky
like a balancing dervish
whirling for a blessing from above?

End of a Marriage

In the vase
edges of tulip petals
browning,
leaves limp,
stalks leaning.

In the vase
there is a spirit
that became old,
trapped
and brittle,
the life that was orange

and yellow and flame.
In this vase
weary stalks
testify to a
loveliness
withering.

My Mooring

I was never good at predictions —
maybe that the lily would open soon,
or the ache in my bones
heralded a rainy evening.
Not that I would be so alone at night
or that I would leave you.

Since then I have lost my touch
with the flowers.
The rain comes and goes with no warning.
Not even the fig tree produced fruit
like last year. Those comforts
have disappeared like puddles under
a harsh sun.

I miss your arms around me, even if
your breath was cold. That mirage
seems like a good thing now:
at least I was able to predict my pain,
which was my mooring.

Poem for an Empty House

You guessed that I went home to an empty house
every day, your eyes two flags at half-mast.
Was I right, you asked, *do you feel lonely?*
I wanted to explain that on my way I stop
to smell honeysuckle hanging over the fence,

neighbors look out kitchen windows to wave,
a Hand of Fatima welcomes at my door.
Later there is a nightly meander to the river,
sometimes a moon rises in the east.
Really, my life is fine, I want to say.

But you knew that my biggest wish
was to open the front door to smells of onion
and garlic frying, a chef at greeting. He would
wrap his apron around my back and draw me near,
salt and pepper in hand, spices for desire. I'd let him

gather me up like swelling dough, exhaling.
Then we'd fall to the floor, two spoons in size order,
clanging. Maybe my undressed eyes tell this story.
Or maybe you're vying for the role of chef,
offering to chop onions and make me weep.

Lingerings

It's not about the pleasure,
not the compass-turning
nor the sun-peak highs
or about my legs tensing
around your torso.

I'm talking about the aftermath
in the hallway
when I cleaned the mud pellets
left from your shoes—
cast off before you unclothed,
after we kissed
and the hours whirred by.

I trace your sojourn
on my hands and knees
like an archaeologist
reconstructing a past—
each artifact excavated,
saved, or lost
after you walked away.

Dinnertime

The forks to probe are where they belong.
The knives for cutting rest on the right.
The spoons for measuring don't know where
to fit, and whether we need them anymore.

Candles with black wicks, flowers
from my garden,

a goblet filled with wine
from Cana, where my father walked.
We can toast my family, Jesus's refugees.

But this feast is about us, you and me.
I invited you to my home, cracks in the plates
and all.

Unexpected Gifts

After a stranger walks by,
a pleasant scent

bright flowering
of forgotten bulbs

fine undulations
behind a slow boat

skin memory
from last night's lovemaking

Waiting

It's the swaying journey of a leaf
from branch to ground

The time for a thought to travel
toward speech

The length of a deep breath
before submerging

The wondrous space
between wakefulness and sleep

Each has forever in it
and an ephemeral rhythm, too

Like your love, sometimes measured
from here to there

Sometimes forgetting itself
between horizons

Traveling with the Speed of Light

News from Damascus scrolls on TV,
a morning chat with a friend just home
from work, seven hours in the future.
My hands can almost touch the cyclamen
on West Bank hills, as if tending flowers
in my backyard. The corniche road
winding around Beirut's tip hugging
the sea, so close to my doorstep.

As world wanderers we click on screens,
sift symbols, look with sister eyes
in oval lenses of intersecting circles,
the radius of the voyage invisible.
Stories between ethereal mouths and
ears, voices in bits and bytes penetrate
thick mountains, deserts. We measure
epiphanies in seconds, move on,

leave unintended footprints:
there are dreams of tented trysts,
shards of conversations, mistakes—
maybe second thoughts—deleted.
Like dense coffee grounds lining once
welcoming cups, or small bowls of dull
olive pits, a sadness. Only scintillas
of thoughts linger, a salty taste in memory.

Now in Washington a white moon blooms
while the sun throws rays on Jerusalem
and Amman…and this luminous language
of loving: imaginary lines around the globe,
a curving cage of messages at the speed
of light. We reach out, draw in, close as
the space between fingers on a keyboard,
far as the great meridian from pole to pole.

بين بين

Acknowledgments

"Colors for the Diaspora" was published in *Lunch Ticket*, January 2018, and in *Making Mirrors: Writing/Righting for and about Refugees*, 2019.

"A Syrian Refugee Speaks" was published in 2019 by *Pleiades* (Volume 39: Issue 1, 2019), in a special tribute to DC Poet Laureate Dolores Kendrick.

"After 93 Years" was published in the anthology, *Write Like You're Alive* (Zoetic Press, 2017). It was selected for publication in *Bettering American Poetry*, Volume 3, 2019.

"Crossing the Mediterranean" was published in the exhibition book for "Water: Trespassing Liquid Highways" at Gallery 102, George Washington University, September-October 2018.

"Syria's Disappeared" was published in *The Fourth River*, Spring 2018.

"Leaving My Childhood Home" was published as Poem of the Week by Split This Rock, February 19, 2016 and in *Making Mirrors: Writing/Righting for and about Refugees*, 2019.

"Immigrant" was published in *Infinite Rust*, Fall 2018.

"Non-Lieux" and "Khayr" were published by *Mizna*, Winter 2019.

"Bayna Bayna, In-Between" was published in *Voice Male*, Fall 2020.

"My Father's Hands" was published in *Heartwood Literary Magazine*, "Poetry—Issue 4," October 1, 2017.

"Learning to Make a Bed" was published by *Passager Journal*, Issue 70, Winter 2021.

"Diving In" was published in *Peace & Identity*, April 2018.

"Losses" and "Dinnertime" were published in *Sukoon Magazine*, Vol. 3, Issue 2, Summer 2015.

"Traveling with the Speed of Light" won the "30 for 30" contest for National Poetry Month, sponsored by *Potomac Review*, April 2018.

I would like to acknowledge and thank friends and family members who have offered unbounded encouragement as I have explored my love for poetry, celebrating with me the small milestones along the way. My deep gratitude goes to my brother Fateh Azzam—my go-to person for invaluable feedback on everything—for his loving support, my sister-in-law Mary McKone for her constant friendship and artistic advice, and to the poet, literary activist, and good friend E. Ethelbert Miller for his generous mentorship. I am so grateful to my wonderful children, Lena and Mark Seikaly, who have always stood by my side.

Special thanks to Shawn Aveningo Sanders for her creative spirit, openness to new ideas, and lovely design and editorial work on this chapbook.

About the Author

Zeina Azzam is a Palestinian American poet, writer, editor, and community activist. She volunteers for organizations that promote Palestinian human rights and the civil rights of vulnerable communities in Alexandria, Virginia, where she lives.

Zeina currently works as publications editor for the think tank, Arab Center Washington DC. Her poems have appeared or are forthcoming in *Passager Journal*, *Pleiades Magazine*, *Cordite Poetry Review*, *Beltway Poetry Quarterly*, *Mizna*, *Sukoon Magazine*, *Split This Rock*, *Heartwood Literary Magazine*, *Lunch Ticket*, *Barzakh: A Literary Magazine*, *The Fourth River*, *Infinite Rust*, and the edited volumes *Tales from Six Feet Apart*, *Bettering American Poetry*, *Making Mirrors: Writing/Righting by and for Refugees*, *Write Like You're Alive*, *The Poeming Pigeon: Love Poems*, *The Poeming Pigeon: Pop Culture*, *Gaza Unsilenced*, and *Yellow as Turmeric, Fragrant as Cloves*. With the poet Sharif Elmusa, Zeina co-translated 14 poems by Arab poets for the Fall 2019 issue of *Loch Raven Review*. She holds an M.A. in Arabic literature from Georgetown University and an M.A. in sociology from George Mason University.

Twitter: @zeina3azzam

Instagram: @zeina.azzam1

About The Poetry Box®

The Poetry Box® is a boutique publishing company in Portland, Oregon, who provides a platform for both established and emerging poets to share their words with the world through beautiful printed books and chapbooks.

Feel free to visit the online bookstore (thePoetryBox.com), where you'll find more titles including:

Matrimony by Laurel Feigenbaum

Nothing More to Lose by Carolyn Martin

Notes from a Caregiver by Meg Lindsay

Like the O in Hope by Jeanne Julian

A Shape of Sky by Cathy Cain

The Very Rich Hours by Gregory Loselle

Just the Girls by Pamela R. Anderson-Bartholet

Between States of Matter by Sherry Rind

The Kingdom of Birds by Joan Colby

Building a Woman by Deborah Meltvedt

My Mother Never Died Before by Marcia B. Loughran

Mouth Quill by Kaja Weeks

and more . . .

بین 50 بین

www.ingramcontent.com/pod-product-compliance
Lightning Source LLC
LaVergne TN
LVHW021054100526
838202LV00083B/5930